30 TIPS TO HEALTHIER RELATIONSHIPS

A guide for couples and anyone else who has relationships to treasure

Jenny Olin, MSW, LCSW

Includes Workbook

Dedication

To my eldest cousin, Bill Bunnell, who, from my earliest memory of him, has modeled for me life's purpose as expressed in Micah 6:8: "O people, the Lord has told you what is good, and this is what he requires of you: to do what is right, to love mercy, and to walk humbly with your God." (NLT)

Acknowledgements

Thank you to the members of Bill O'Hanlon's *Next Level* Group for their encouragement while writing this book, and to Bill for generously sharing his knowledge and experience each step of the way. Thanks also to Emily Muller, Esq, for legal comment, Reverends Bonita Bates and Deborah Rose for their valued reflections, Sandy Beadle for her excellent technical assistance, and my faithful feline Joy for good-naturedly keeping me company through marathons at the keyboard. It takes a lot of support to see even a small book through from beginning to end.

"Royalty-Free Clip Art Images" Clip Art Designs © Graphics Factory. Used with full legal rights. www.GraphicsFactory.com.

Table of Contents

How To Use This Book

You probably opened this book curious to know what it has to offer about having a healthier relationship with someone. You want to succeed. I want you to succeed. Too this end, (risking overuse of the word) I've included some tips for using these tips.

Suggestions for using this book successfully:
- Read all the tips.
- Choose a tip to improve a relationship using one of these options.
  - Start with the first tip.
  - Start with a tip that inspires you – gives you hope and energy.
  - Start with a tip with which you expect to experience immediate success.
  - Start with a tip that addresses your greatest relationship concern.
- Use the workbook in the second section of this book to try out this tip.
- Practice the tip until you have "nailed" it, and made it a new habit.
- Continue using this tip and choose another to practice for relationship health.

You may have a method that works better for you. Great! Use it!

Recommendations for what not to do.
- Avoid skipping a tip because you think it might be useless or irrelevant.
- Avoid learning more than one tip at a time. It can be a way to set yourself up for failure.
- Avoid pushing this book on someone else, telling him or her they should use these tips, too.

Recommendations for what to do.
- Choose a small step you can do now to improve a relationship.
- If you discover the step you choose to take is too big, break it down into smaller steps. Small successes add up to big ones.
- Repeat what works.
- Stop doing what doesn't work and revise your plan.
- Stay with it. Resist giving up.
- Use the workbook. If you don't want to write in this book, write in a notebook or journal.
- Ask a trusted friend to help you be accountable, stay on track, and when needed, get unstuck. You don't have to do this alone.

30 Tips to Healthier Relationships gives you great tools to create healthier relationships with your spouse or someone else who is significant in your life. It is not intended to be psychotherapy or counseling, or to replace psychotherapy or counseling.

TIP #1
Share verbal appreciation every day.

Sharing appreciation every day using words is a great place to start strengthening a relationship. We like to hear genuine compliments and thanks. Sharing appreciations this way also helps us remember what we like about a person.

Experiment with expanding your verbal expressions of appreciation. If you are a person of few words, you might find this challenging at first. It is something you can learn to do. Like learning most skills, it gets easier with practice.

We like to hear genuine compliments and thanks.

Try this formula:
1. State your appreciation.
2. In a few short sentences, say why you have this appreciation.

Here are two examples:

OK: "I appreciate your making dinner tonight."
GREAT: "I appreciate your making dinner tonight. Driving home from work, I had no idea what to cook. When I walked in the door and discovered you were already cooking, I felt huge relief! Thank you so much! I love you!"

OK: "I appreciate you not giving me a hard time about going out with the guys last night."
GREAT: "I appreciate you not giving me a hard time about going out with the guys last night. I know you weren't interested in going to the hockey game, and I really wanted to see it. I needed the break in routine. After the game, it was nice to come home and crawl into bed next to you."

Practice keeping your appreciations clear and to the point. If you take longer than 30 – 40 seconds to share one, it is probably too long. Find a balance between enough words and too many words. Using too many words can dilute your message. Also, if your message is too long, the receiver may stop listening and won't hear your appreciation.

Be sure to keep your appreciations real. We usually see through fake ones.

What verbal appreciation(s) will you share today?

TIP #2
Recognize and share non-verbal appreciation.

In Tip #1, you learned about sharing appreciation with words. Another way to share appreciation is non-verbally, that is, without words. It adds value to relationships when each person can express and receive both verbal and non-verbal appreciations.

It is easy to miss non-verbal appreciations if we expect words. Non-verbal appreciations challenge us in a different way than learning what words to say. The challenge is learning how to show appreciations successfully through action, and how to recognize them when they are given to us.

The following are two examples of non-verbal appreciation:

After sex, Jim says nothing, but embraces his wife, Ann, with warmth and tenderness. His non-verbal message is "I appreciate you having sex with me tonight. I know you are tired and you made the effort for me. With this hug, I'm saying 'I noticed,' 'thank you' and 'I love you.'"

Your teenage son washes and waxes your car. The unspoken message is "thanks for the advice you gave me on how to interview for the job at the electronics store. I sure am going to like this job better than the one I had washing dishes at the restaurant."

A non-verbal appreciation given in a timely and direct response to something is easier for the receiver to identify than one given hours or days later. Delivery matters. In the first example above, although tired and ready for sleep, Ann chooses to have sex with Jim. If he hugs her warmly before they fall asleep, and Ann recognizes non-verbal messages, she receives Jim's appreciation. If he waits until the next evening to cook dinner to show his appreciation, Ann may or may not connect the dots between the two events. If Jim waits several days to cook dinner to show his appreciation, odds are much lower Ann will make the connection. The longer the delay in expressing non-verbal appreciation, the harder it is for the recipient to recognize the connection. An unrecognized non-verbal appreciation is a breakdown in communication.

Be a detective by practicing your observation and interpretation skills. Watch and wait. It is easy to miss non-verbal appreciations if we expect words. If we don't receive verbal appreciations and are not recognizing non-verbal ones, we are likely to feel unhappiness or despair. We might believe who we are or what we do isn't valued, noticed, or loved. How wrong we can be!

How will you show non-verbal appreciation today? Will you look for non-verbal expressions of appreciation given to you today?

TIP #3

When someone talks to you, focus on what he or she is saying.

Hearing another person speak without listening to what he or she is saying, is something many of us do much more often than we realize or want to admit.

Not listening happens for many reasons. Two significant ones are:

1. believing we know what the speaker is going to say, so we find no reason to listen, and
2. turning to our own thoughts in preparation to respond to the speaker.

When we know someone for a while, we may think we can predict what he or she will say next. Impatience and/or assumption lead us to believe we know the ending. While it is possible we are right, it is also possible we are wrong. Commonly we stop paying adequate attention to the speaker; we tune them out. Communication breaks down when what we believe we will hear is not what is said.

When you focus on listening to your own thoughts, you cannot be a good listener to someone else.

Related, when someone is talking on a topic about which we expect to disagree, we tend to stop listening instead of hearing his or her point of view. We tune the speaker out and focus our thoughts on planning our counterpoint. When you focus on listening to your own thoughts, you cannot be a good listener to someone else. How will you know for sure you hear someone correctly if you are not listening attentively?

Some people believe they can multi-task listening and planning their response at the same time. In reality, it doesn't work well. Listening becomes impaired when we divide our attention.

Sometimes two people argue, unaware they agree with each other. This happens when neither listens to what the other says. They both assume disagreement and create conflict where none existed.

What is your experience when someone tunes you out and makes assumptions about what you say? Is this an experience you want to create for someone else?

Are you ready to have fewer unnecessary arguments due to misunderstandings? Will you focus on hearing accurately what is said to you?

What will you do to practice being a better listener today?

TIP #4

Treat another's concerns seriously.

Accept the worries of others, even when you cannot relate to them. Discounting someone's concern because you don't understand or can't relate to it blocks connection in your relationship.

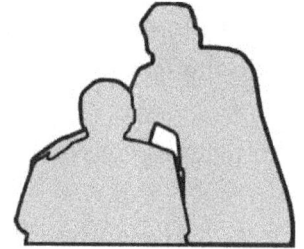

Since it is impossible to know exactly the inner path someone else is traveling, we cannot fully know his or her experience. We can, perhaps, come close or make a good guess, but we will never truly *know*.

We are not in a position to pass judgment on the importance or validity of someone else's distress. We may not see the reason for someone's concern. Even if we can't, it *is* their concern. Discounting, mocking, or criticizing a person for their unease can be shortsighted, thoughtless, and just plain mean. It hurts both the other person and your relationship.

We may not see the reason for someone's concern. Even if we can't, it is their concern.

Do you remember a time when you had a concern that was not taken seriously? Maybe you were told you shouldn't feel what you feel or had no right to how you felt. Maybe you were mocked for your concern. What did you think? What did you feel? What do you wish the other person had done differently? These are important questions to think about. You can use them to help you choose how you react to other people's concerns.

What concern are you not accepting in someone you value because you don't understand it or can't relate? Will you stop and listen to their distress today and acknowledge it is real to him or her?

TIP #5

Ask permission, and get it, before offering advice.

Ugh, almost no one likes unsolicited advice, no matter how good it is. Most of us have, or think we have, great advice to offer at least now and then. We've been there, done that. Or, from a distance, the solution seems obvious.

Your advice may be right on target. No matter how right you are, experienced you are, insightful you are, or how good your idea is, if someone is not ready to hear it, your counsel won't help. Instead, it could hurt your relationship. It is a way to create conflict and distance between you and another person.

Typical reactions to unsolicited advice are anger, starting a fight, withdrawal, feeling stupid, or purposefully doing something unhealthy. These reactions apply to both the giver and receiver. They are not the goals of advice giving!

Ask first if someone wants your advice – to hear what you have to say. If the answer is "no," don't give it. This can be incredibly hard to do! Excuse yourself from the situation if needed, to stop from giving the advice. Wait. This person may come to you later, when he or she is ready, to ask what your advice is.

No matter how right you are... if someone is not ready to hear it, your counsel won't help.

When an adult hasn't given you permission to butt in, it is in both your best interests to butt out. (Consider immediate danger and medical emergencies two exceptions to asking for permission to give advice.)

If you want to offer advice today, will you ask for and wait for permission before you give it?

11

TIP #6
Practice goodwill.

A mean spirit hurts both others and you.

You don't have to "get religion" to value the advice from the Golden Rule: "In everything, therefore, treat people the same way you want them to treat you" (Matthew 7:12, NAS). By consistently showing goodwill (interest, concern, support) towards your partner, you help set a tone – create an environment – for kindness, friendship, trust, and genuine intimacy. By showing goodwill, you live an example that often is both reciprocated and passed on to someone else.

> ... "In everything, therefore, treat people the same way you want them to treat you" (Matthew 7:12, NAS).

Showing goodwill towards another individual has the potential for exponential growth for promoting it in our families, workplaces, schools, places of worship, neighborhoods and communities, our country, and our world. You have the potential for a whole lot of positive influence when you make the decision to practice goodwill as a lifestyle.

What act(s) of goodwill will you do today?

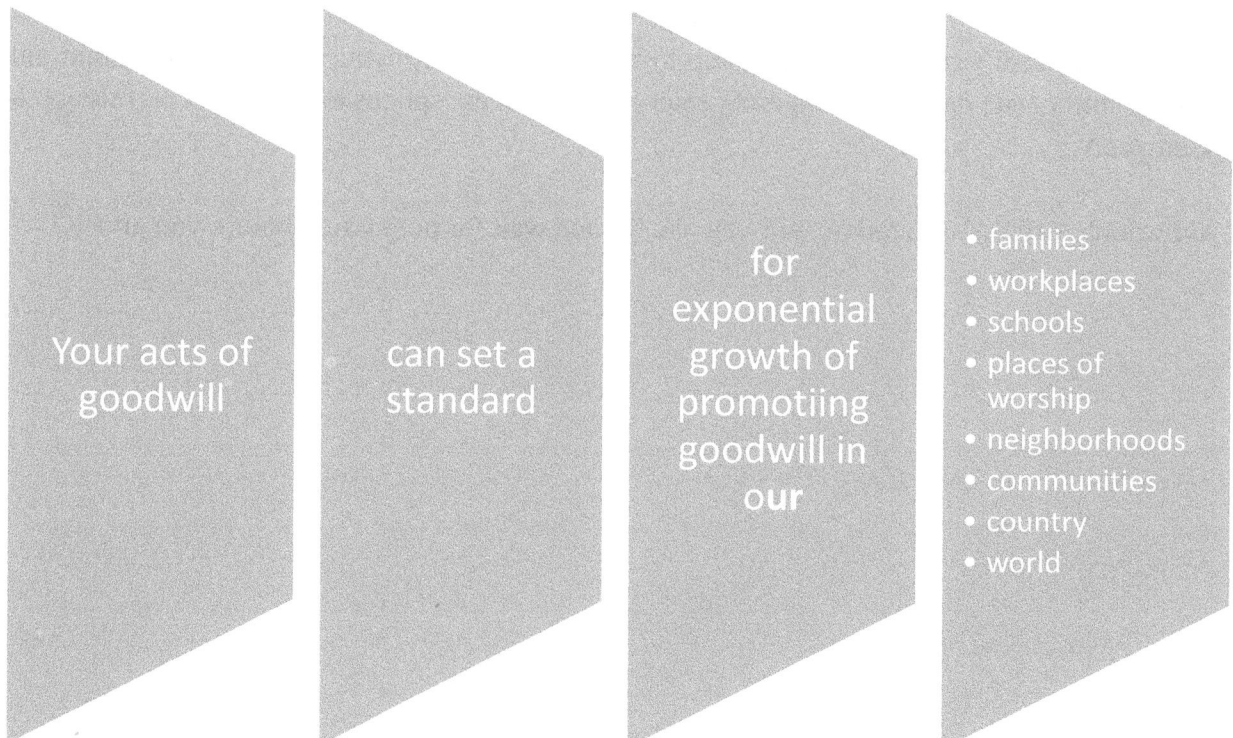

Your acts of goodwill

can set a standard

for exponential growth of promotiing goodwill in our

- families
- workplaces
- schools
- places of worship
- neighborhoods
- communities
- country
- world

TIP #7
Make choices based on what you value. rather than what you feel.

We have feelings in response to what we are experiencing (thinking, doing, happening to us) in the moment. Feelings can change rapidly and frequently and may not be consistent over time.

Values, in part, are what is important to us. They are what we treasure and cherish, and are our standards for what is right and wrong. Values, while they may change during a lifetime, tend to be highly consistent over years and decades.

Consider Amy, an elementary school girl, who becomes upset when her longest and best friend Erin plays with someone else at recess. Amy's feelings are hurt and she decides from her hurt place Erin is no longer her best friend. The next day, Erin plays with Amy at recess and sits with her at lunch. Amy forgets yesterday's hurt. They are still best friends. The *feelings* from the previous day pass, but the lasting *value* of their friendship survives Amy's crisis.

As adults, we not only have feelings in reaction to the present moment, we also have them in response to memories and in anticipation of the future. If we are not careful, our feelings – particularly those of anger, hurt, fear, and sadness – can take over and we lose sight of our values.

In a troubled relationship, we often become caught up in our negative feelings when responding to the situation. We forget the value we have received in the relationship. We forget we are friends, not enemies. Our feelings snowball and overshadow our values. Those feelings can deceive us. They can prevent us from remembering why we chose this relationship

We forget we are friends, not enemies.

and from remembering why we value it. When your feelings and values clash, staying with your values keeps you on the right track.

Do you have a relationship in which you are currently discounting its long-term value because your feelings are getting in the way of tuning in to what you value? What is one thing you will do differently today to help you get back in touch with what you value in this relationship?

Today will you make or renew the choice to live by your values rather than by your feelings?

TIP #8
Be careful on Facebook.

Many people currently consider Facebook one of the most boundariless places in existence.

Facebook can be an opportunity for friends to find and reconnect with each other. Families connect easier because everyone has access to the same information.

However, many people have and are putting their relationships in jeopardy because of who they "Friend" and what they indiscreetly or thoughtlessly post on Facebook.

Also, old flames are rekindling and new ones are lighting. Perhaps connection is innocent at first. But as you will see in Tip #15: *Express complaints privately,* subtle steps can gradually lead to emotional and physical affairs.

Since Facebook and other social media sites have become popular, relationship psychotherapists report a startling increase in the number of people seeking help resolving trust issues stemming from affairs and other unhealthy personal interactions. While acknowledging additional contributing factors to increasing trust issues in relationships, they attribute much of it as originating with Internet social media contact.

Protect yourself and your important relationships. If you don't want the world to know something, don't put it on Facebook. If you are already in a relationship with someone and connect with an old friend of the opposite gender, tell your partner. Be completely open about it. You may need to remove some, maybe most or all, of these people from your "Friend" list so they are removed from your temptation list.

Many people currently consider Facebook one of the most boundariless places in existence.

Use social networking to your health and not to your destruction. Educate yourself well about how Facebook and other social media work, and learn how to stay updated with site policy changes.

What do you need to remove from your Facebook pages today? Whom do you need to remove from your "Friend" list today? Will you commit to these actions?

TIP #9

Make having satisfying relationships a priority over being right.

We like to be right. It feels good. However, being right isn't a priority in healthy personal relationships. Insisting on being right can hurt relationships.

Insisting you are right can contribute to feelings of inadequacy in the other person, and to disagreements and defensiveness, creating an atmosphere of tension and ill will. Each contributes to emotional distance. If these are consequences of being right, how do they affect your desire to win at the *"I'm right"* game?

Remember Tip #7 *Make choices based on what you value, rather than what you feel*? You may *feel* like proving you are right, although your *value* may be healthy personal relationships. When you value and practice promoting and nurturing goodwill (see Tip # 6 *Practice Goodwill*), you focus on a choice to support others in feeling adequate. You help create emotional closeness.

Does this mean you should say you are wrong when you believe you are right? No. What you *can* do is hold back from pushing your belief onto someone else. Let them have his or her opinion. Acknowledge their point of view.

Being right is not a "win" if it hurts a relationship.

Being right is not a "win" if it hurts a relationship. When you put your energy towards the health of your relationship, both you and your relationship win.

Think about it. Would you rather be right or would you rather be happy, close, and connected with your spouse or other significant relationship? What action step will you take towards your choice today?

15

TIP #10
Look for the exceptions to problems.

"Is your glass half empty or half full?" Most people are familiar with this question.

When we have a problem that keeps repeating, it is normal to feel discouraged, angry, and/or scared. We can develop a negative attitude. We spend our energy focused on our glass being half-empty instead of half-full. We focus so much attention on what is wrong, we fail to see exceptions, that is, the times when the problem could happen, but is not happening. When our focus stays on when the problem occurred, is occurring, or will occur again, our emotions send us into a downward spiral. Simply stated, things get worse.

Fortunately, we have an option. Few situations are rarely the extremes of "always" or "never" we assign to them. We can look for, and find, exceptions to a problem – the times when the problem does not occur.

A baby who cries most of the time doesn't *always* cry, although it may seem this way. When you look for the exceptions when the baby isn't crying, your "always" belief disappears. Then, by discovering what is different during those times, you have the **We can look for, and find, exceptions to a problem...** opportunity to choose to create an environment that lessens the baby's need to cry. When you do, your emotions and the situation begin to spiral up. Things improve.

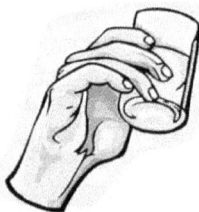

When you have a recurring problem in a relationship, look for the times when the problem normally might have happened, but does not happen. Look for what is different about the way you act, the way you think, and/or the situation during the times the problem doesn't happen. Notice what changes when you focus your attention on these exceptions.

After you find an exception to the way you act, the way you think, and/or the situation, create the exception again. Repeat what you discover works most of the time, even if it doesn't work *all* the time. Do this instead of repeating what hasn't worked most or all of the time.

Once you identify even one exception, you can begin to see your glass as half full. Once you change how you think about or act on the problem to recreate that exception, you create the space for the exception to happen again. When you make the exception the rule, you eliminate the problem!

What exceptions to a problem are you willing to notice and recreate today?

TIP #11
Be trustworthy.

Being trustworthy isn't just for Abraham Lincoln or Boy Scouts. Trust is essential in a healthy relationship.

You know what you can say or do to break trust. You can do it in an instant. Sadly, repairing what you can do in an instant to break a trust can take years to restore.

Since you know what to do to break trust, you know what to do to keep trust. It can be helpful to make a list of what to do to show you are trustworthy. This list will help you start.

- Keep your word – do what you say you will do.
- If you are not certain you can say "yes" to a request, say so and then take time to decide.
- Be open in your most important relationships – refrain from lying, hiding information, or telling only part of the story.
- Answer questions without defensiveness.
- If you don't want to share something, say so directly rather than be evasive.
- Tell the truth in a loving way.

Trust is essential in a healthy relationship. Broken trust is one of the hardest relationship problems to heal. It takes countless repeated proof of trustworthiness, great patience, and staying power to recover from broken trust. One slip-up, or perceived slip-up, can send healing back several steps. Even with an excellent track record, doubt and fear of another incident can linger for years. Years later, an unrelated incident can trigger the memory of broken trust, causing a temporary setback. It is painful and frustrating.

Do you feel discouraged or hopeless after reading about the difficulties restoring trust? If you do, remember this: restoring broken trust is not hopeless. Healing can and does happen when a solid plan of accountability is in place and followed. Restoring trust can create a relationship that is stronger and more committed than before the break in trust.

If you haven't broken trust with your partner, hopefully this convinces you not to break it. If you have broken trust with your partner, do the hard work of healing the smart way.

What will you do to be trustworthy today?

TIP #12
Avoid blaming.

In relationships, finger pointing – playing *The Blame Game* – has little value. What does have value is using healthy, successful problem-solving skills to end conflict and prevent it from happening again.

This is similar to Tip #9 *Make having satisfying relationships a priority over being right.* Ask yourself, would you rather spend your time and energy pointing out someone's faults and the part they play in the problem, or put your time and energy into being part of the solution and creating satisfying closeness?

In relationships finger pointing - playing The Blame Game - has little value.

Where you focus your attention is going to determine the result you get. Blame places one of you in the victim role or turns into a game of tit-for-tat. As in Tip #10 *Look for the exceptions to problems,* whatever went wrong in the first place will spiral further downward. Instead of blaming, seek out a healthy solution to solve the conflict, and experience an upward spiral.

To blame or not to blame – that is the question. It's your choice. What is your answer to this question today?

TIP #13
Look for the best in people.

When you focus on the good in others, their strengths stand out. Their flaws become smaller.

Where you decide to focus your attention determines what you will see. When you look for what is unlikable about a person, the more negative things you will find. A pattern of finding faults leads to finding more faults, even inventing some.

When you look for what is agreeable in a person, the more positive things you will find. You develop an eye for focusing on what you like about him or her.

That said, use good sense. If, for instance, you discover the person you are dating is a drug addict, wisdom says to pay attention to this negative. Seeing the good in someone does not mean it is a healthy choice for you to become involved in a serious relationship with him or her.

You can influence yours and others' moods and attitudes with your point of view. Make the center of your attention someone's flaws and you help create and support a negative atmosphere. You and people around you feel worse. Make the center of attention someone's good points and you help create and maintain a pleasant atmosphere. You and people around you feel better. Try it.

When you look for what is agreeable in a person, the more positive things you will find.

Will you spend today looking for the good in everyone you meet?

TIP #14

Take a time out.

While disagreements and misunderstandings in relationships are inevitable, how you handle them makes the difference between having a positive or a negative outcome. For a positive outcome, take a "time out" when you need it.

1. Call a "time out" when overly aroused. When we become upset, our heart rate and blood pressure go up and stress hormones surge through our bodies. This is called "arousal." A little arousal can be energizing – motivation to deal with a problem. Too much arousal is harmful, not only in our relationships, but also to our emotional and physical health.

When you find yourself in "fight," "flight," or "freeze" mode (overly aroused) in a situation that is not life-threatening, odds are overwhelmingly high you will respond in an unhealthy, ineffective manner. (A concrete way to measure too much arousal is when you are upset and your heart rate goes above 90-95 beats per minute.) You set yourself up for a negative outcome if you try to resolve a conflict while overly aroused.

When you are overly aroused, spend 20-30 minutes doing something to distract yourself from thinking about what is upsetting you. You need at least that much time to let your body physically quiet down from its aroused state. Removing yourself from the conflict is not enough. The key is to *distract* yourself from thinking about whatever triggered your arousal. Your body will stay on high alert as long as you continue to think about the problem and how upset you feel.

Proven effective steps to take:
1. Call a "time out" when overly aroused.
2. Tell the person with whom you are in conflict you will return in 30 minutes.
3. Distract yourself for that length of time. Do and think about something other than the problem or another arousing situation.
4. Keep your commitment to return in 30 minutes.
5. Start over to resolve the conflict from a non-aroused or lower-aroused place. Avoid repeating what didn't work before. Many tips in this book offer alternatives.
6. Repeat steps 1-5 as necessary until you achieve a positive outcome.

If you become overly aroused today, will you choose to work towards a positive outcome and follow these time-out steps?

TIP #15
Express complaints privately.

Avoid criticizing anyone, present or absent, publically. Share complaints privately and directly to the individual. Public criticism is an expression of ill will.

Common occasions when public criticism tends to occur include when we
- feel unable to contain our frustration, hurt, or anger, i.e., our arousal level is too high (see Tip #14 *Take a time out* for dealing with high arousal levels), or
- have drunk too much alcohol or used other substances to the extent enough access to the rational part of our brain is lost.

When someone criticizes you where others can hear, avoid taking your turn at publically pointing out his or her flaws, or otherwise acting mean-spirited (see Tip #12 *Avoid blaming*). An alternative is to use Tip #6 *Practice Goodwill*. Four options for practicing goodwill include
- keep quiet,
- change the subject,
- respond with a kind word and/or action, or
- quietly remove yourself from the situation.

Expressing complaints privately is of added importance for couples in committed relationships. If you criticize or complain about your partner in public, you advertise your unhappiness. Although it may be temporary discontent, others might interpret this as a signal you are available for a new relationship. You put yourself in a vulnerable spot to be approached by someone interested in you. While you may think you will never stray, resolve can break down small bits at a time until you discover you have made a series of bad choices, ending in an emotional and/or physical affair. Temptation often attacks in small, subtle steps.

Public criticism is an expression of ill will.

Each one of us has a choice. By our thoughts, words, and actions we contribute either to the positive or to the negative aspects of our relationships and our society.

Do you have a complaint worth expressing to someone? Will you choose to express it privately rather than publically today?

TIP #16

Make your most important relationship a higher priority than you.

When your relationship wins, you both win. How can this be true when two people have different wants? He wants to watch football. She wants to show him the pamphlets she picked up at the Travel Agency and talk about where to go on vacation.

How do you both win? Perhaps reluctantly at first, because he hates missing a game, he will acknowledge the relationship with his partner is more important than the football game. Perhaps too, in spite of how much she looks forward to an exciting vacation, she will admit their relationship is more important than pushing vacation brochures at him.

When, together, you nurture and nourish your relationship, your relationship wins.

But she wonders "can't he miss ONE football game and talk to me?" He wonders "can't I watch this game now and talk about vacation LATER?" In both cases, of course!

Who has a higher priority? Neither. Your relationship has the higher priority. When, together, you nurture and nourish your relationship, your relationship wins. You both feel you are getting enough. You both believe you win. Then the football game vs. vacation plans is no longer an issue, because it never was the issue. The issue is the value you demonstrate you have for your relationship.

What will you do today to make your relationship a higher priority than you? If you are saying, "if only he/she would…" you aren't focusing on the question. Have another go at it: what will *you* do today to make your relationship a higher priority than you?

TIP #17

When you make a mistake, ask for forgiveness.

Giving a gift is one way people try to "make up" after making a mistake. It is a request to overlook a behavior.

The second part of restitution is asking for forgiveness. Flowers, new golf clubs, jewelry, or some other longed-for object given with the belief it will fix or make up for a mistake, does not create relationship health. A gift lacks value when given with the intention to repair a goof or bad behavior. The gift doesn't fix anything and becomes a reminder of the wrong that was done. Who wants that kind of memory?

Compare this to gifts received for celebrations or for no reason. These gifts create lasting memories of pleasure and joy.

What is the remedy for a mistake? While saying "I'm sorry" helps, it is only one part of making restitution (making amends). Too often, we say "I'm sorry" without correcting our actions.

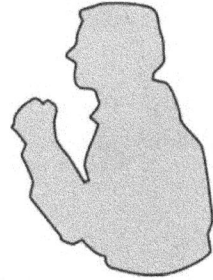

The second part of restitution is asking for forgiveness. You may not receive forgiveness right away. Still, it is important to ask.

The third part of restitution is not repeating the mistake – promoting trust (see Tip #11 *Be trustworthy)*.

What kind of memories do you want associated with your gifts? What have you said or done for which you need to ask forgiveness today?

TIP #18
Start chain reactions of positive events.

Have you ever set up a row of dominos standing close together on end as in the picture below, and then gently tipping over the first one, watching them fall in sequence one after the other? Tipping the first domino begins a chain reaction that continues until the last one has tipped and fallen. It's fascinating!

The domino effect happens in relationships. One small action sets off a chain reaction of either positive or negative events. One small action can have a big influence on the direction a relationship takes.

Try an experiment. Come home and make a mean comment to whoever is around when you walk in the door. What happens next? And next? And next? Or, better yet, greet him or her with a smile and kind words when you walk in the door. What happens next? And next? And next?

YOU can make the first move... Watch the chain reaction of positive events follow.

You do not have to do all the work to make a relationship better. YOU can make the first move by nudging the first relationship domino so it tips in the right direction. Watch the chain reaction of positive events follow. It's fascinating!

You are in a powerful position. In your interaction with all people, when you stop and think before you speak or act, you have limitless opportunities to tip the first domino in a positive direction.

Where and how will you "tip the first domino" and start a chain reaction of positive events today?

TIP #19
Practice good sleep habits.

Seventy-four percent of North Americans are seriously sleep deprived, and most of them don't even know it. Nearly all North Americans have some sleep deprivation.[1]

Tiredness often leads to bad moods, short tempers, miscommunication, arguing, withdrawal, depression, anxiety, inflexibility, and a lot of other troublesome experiences to trigger negative reactions and communication with others.

Seventy-four percent of North Americans are seriously sleep deprived... Most people don't consider the harmful impact sleep deprivation has on our relationships. Chronic tiredness can contribute to relationships falling apart. When we consistently get enough of the *right kind* of sleep (REM and Stage 4 sleep), we can have major improvement in how we get along with others. Overcoming sleep deprivation can even prevent break-ups and divorce.

You may think the practices for restorative sleep are unrelated to having a better relationship. Research shows they clearly do.[2] However, many proven successful routines and tools for a good night's sleep run counter to our lifestyle choices. These choices alone can explain why we are sleep deprived.

Here are some of the top healthy sleep practices:
- Drink no caffeine after 2 PM.
- Avoid evening alcohol.
- Keep electronics out of the bedroom.
- Turn off computers and TV an hour before bed.
- Go to bed and get up at the same time seven days a week.
- Get at least eight hours of sleep every night.
- Sleep on a supportive mattress and pillow.

What is one or more healthy sleep practice you are willing to creatively put into action and begin overcoming your sleep deprivation today?

---

[1] Personal interview February 8, 2010 with James Maas, PhD, the world's leading sleep researcher and educator.
[2] See footnote 1.

TIP #20
Avoid resentments.

To avoid resentments, set healthy boundaries. Say "yes" when you mean yes; say "no" when you mean no.

A boundary is the place where one thing ends and another thing begins. The end of the last sentence and the beginning of this sentence is a boundary. A fence dividing your lawn and your neighbor's is a boundary. Where your skin ends and the rest of the world begins is a boundary. Got it?

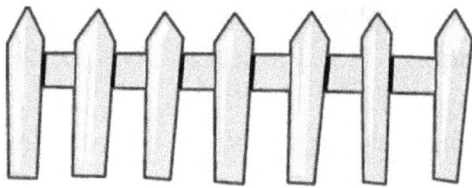

Those are examples of external or outer boundaries. We have boundaries inside ourselves, too. Where we stop one thought and start another, is an internal boundary. Where we separate what we value from what we feel, is an internal boundary (see Tip #7 *Make choices based on what you value, rather than what you feel.*)

When you say "yes" to something you don't want to do, that is ignore your boundaries, you can count on feeling some level of conflict inside you. When this happens, you either dig in your heels and don't do what you say you will do, or you do it with resentment. You might hide your resentment, or in some way take it out on the person making the request or on someone else who is in your line of fire.

When you choose real giving, your initial "no" changes to a loving, resentment-free "yes."

A healthy goal is to have what you experience inside of you match what you say and do on the outside. Your inside "yes" matches your outside "yes". Your inside "no" matches your outside "no." When you feel free to say "no," it is surprising how much more often you choose to say "yes."

Part of "real giving" is when you give to someone what he or she wants, whether or not you understand their want. When you choose real giving, your initial "no" changes to a loving, resentment-free "yes."

Where in your life today do you need to say "no" in your head and with your voice and actions to avoid resentment and free you up to say more "yeses?" How can you turn your resentful "no" into a loving "yes" today?

TIP # 21
Choose the best time to bring up a problem.

Set your relationship up for the best possible resolution to conflict. Your timing of when you bring up a problem can make the difference between a positive and a negative outcome.

Some bad times to bring up a problem are:
- when the other person is walking out the door,
- when the other person walks in the door,
- when either one of you is exhausted,
- when you don't have permission from the other person to talk about it,
- when the other person is doing something else,
- meal time,
- after a pleasant evening out,
- when the children distract you,
- during work,
- during the other's favorite TV show, and
- at bedtime.

A lot of bad times to bring up a problem exist.

Choose a time and a place agreed upon together, when you are free from outside distractions that pull your focus away...

This begs the question, when is a good time? Choose a time and a place agreed upon together, when you are free from outside distractions that pull your focus away from your conversation. Talk when you are both calm and not aroused (see Tip #14 *Take a time out*).

Some people believe a good time to bring up a problem does not exist. It is probably not true, but if it seems true, avoid the worst times. You might use the list above as a guide.

If you need to bring up a problem with someone, when would be some good times? If you don't think of any, will you become an active observer today to discover what options are available you have overlooked or discounted, and try them?

TIP #22

Live from this day forward.

Avoid letting past problems and traumas define who you are today.

We can use our past to explain why we are the way we are now, and blame it for why we have the relationship problems we have today. If we allow it, old baggage has a way of colliding with, and spoiling the present. We can spend years in individual and relationship therapy analyzing how past experiences affect our choices today. Or, we can take action to separate our negative past from the present, and decide to leave those experiences in the past where they belong.

Here's a tool you can use. Imagine you carry a huge, heavy pack filled with your past. In your imagination, draw a thick, long line in the sand to divide the past from the present. On the "past" side of the line, set down your pack, open and empty it. Check to make sure you didn't leave anything inside!

Take a good look at everything that was in your pack. Set aside any contents interfering with fully participating in healthy relationships today. Thank them sincerely for any purpose they once served, and tell them you no longer need or want them. Say goodbye to the problems and trauma from your past. Take as much time as you need.

Carefully repack all your good memories and successful tools. Give thanks for them. Then pick up your pack. Notice how much lighter it is. When you are ready, step over the line you drew in the sand separating your past from your present. Focus on looking forward. You won't wipe the past from your memory, but you can have it be a memory rather than a heavy burden you carry, hurting you and the relationships in your life today.

This is a new day. You can choose how you live it, regardless of what has come before.

If you don't know what to do now that you have left the past behind, stay on the "present" side of your line and do nothing. Wait patiently. Doing nothing creates space and time to allow something new and healthy to happen.

This is a new day. You can choose how you live it, *regardless of what has come before.* No matter what happened in your past, you are responsible for making healthy choices today.

Do you need to draw a line in the sand and cross over to the present, taking this step to free you for healthier relationships? Whatever your answer, what will you do today to live from this day forward?

TIP #23
Be a successful mind reader.

Successful mind reading happens when you check out the accuracy of your mind reading.

Whether you have experienced emotional closeness (openness) with someone, or simply spent a long time with a person, you become accustomed to his or her patterns. You believe you can predict their thoughts and actions. And, in many cases, you *can* accurately read his or her mind because you are accustomed to their patterns.

When a person's inaccurate mind reading goes unchecked, it creates disconnection in relationships...

Mind reading is risky business, though. Patterns are not followed 100% of the time. Exceptions happen.

When a person's inaccurate mind reading goes unchecked, it creates disconnection in relationships through *avoidable* misunderstanding. This can lead to anger, hopelessness, despair, resentment, and a whole lot of other painful feelings and experiences. Yet many people repeatedly mind read despite the harm it does to relationships.

This tip is really a warning not to read minds. Instead, find out if what you believe is true, partly true, or not true. Here's a way to do it.

- Let your partner know you want to check something out with him or her.
- Ask if this is a good time.
- If the answer is "no," *do not continue,* no matter how badly you want to check it out! Stay calm and wait. Many times partners will ask you later what it is you want to know. If they don't, choose your time carefully and ask again. You can use the suggestions in Tip #21 *Choose the best time to bring up a problem.*
- If you get a green light, use a calm, conversational tone to ask if what you are thinking your partner is thinking is true. If it is, you have confirmed your belief.
- If it is partly true or not true, continue in a calm voice to ask what is true. When your partner responds, you have the information you need.

This tool works well because it prevents misunderstandings and using unnecessary negative energy. Instead, it provides a structure for clear, accurate communication.

Will you try out this mind reading tool today?

29

TIP #24
Spend quality time together.

Getting and keeping quality emotional connection requires spending time together. While this is a no-brainer, too many couples don't make quality time a priority. They insist they don't have time in their schedules. A surprising number of couples claim the recommendation to spend 10 to 15 minutes a day sharing their appreciations, new information, questions, concerns, requests, hopes, and dreams with each other is unreasonable!

Conversation may take place around their children's activities, extended family needs, gossip, and disagreements, but not on topics that support the health of the couple's relationship. Ignoring nurturing a committed relationship is a setup for it to fall apart.

Getting and keeping quality emotional connection requires spending time together. Some people avoid finding time because they are uncomfortable sitting face to face, eye to eye, when talking about their relationship. Research of gender differences shows men are more likely to talk quality relationship talk when they are in action and/or when continuous eye contact is not required.

One of these suggestions may ease discomfort when sit-down relationship talk overwhelms someone.

- Take a walk together. (Added benefits of walking are the positive effects aerobic exercise has on heart health, mood, and brainpower. See Tip #26 *Exercise regularly.*)
- Go for a drive.
- Talk on the phone.

Where do you find the time?

- Discontinue gossiping and arguing. (Review tips throughout this book for ways to discontinue arguing.)
- Watch less TV.
- Spend less at-home time on the computer.
- Put the kids to bed on time.

Make just one of these changes and you will have time to talk.

What will you do today to begin or continue spending quality time connecting in your most important relationship?

TIP #25
Take a break from your relationship problem.

When you can do nothing about a relationship problem in the moment, take a break from it. Set it aside for a while.

Living a problem 24/7 is exhausting. Unresolved issues can interfere with concentration, keep you unnecessarily isolated, continue an unproductive, elevated level of emotional arousal, reinforce and increase the size of a negative point of view, and keep you awake at night.

Taking a break to restore ourselves often helps us get a clearer and fresher point of view.

Taking a break to restore ourselves often helps us get a clearer and fresher point of view. It can help put a problem in perspective. It doesn't mean it has gone away. But life is more than problems. When we have some serious ones, we tend to forget this.

Calling a truce during a relationship problem and doing something pleasurable together reminds us we can enjoy each other. Consider having a date where you agree not to discuss the problem before, during, or right after your date. Time away from a disagreement may reduce conflict simply because you remember you really do like each other. Having a diversion in the midst of conflict or crisis, even having some fun together, may become a significant step in the solution.

It's a good idea to take a problem break when:
- you are stuck and can see no reasonable solution,
- you're too tired to deal with the problem and each other effectively,
- one or both person's emotional arousal level is too high (see Tip #14 *Take a time out)* to problem-solve effectively (when in doubt, assume it is),
- your problem-solving approach is making the situation worse, not better,
- you need facts unavailable at that time to reach a solution, and/or
- problem-solving stops being productive and you can't figure out what to do differently.

It is also time to move your focus away from a problem when you have reached a solution you cannot put into action until a later time. Congratulate each other on having a plan. Then set the problem aside until it is time to take your planned action.

Whether or not you are currently struggling with a relationship problem, will you invite your spouse or another significant person in your life to do something fun with you today?

TIP #26
Exercise regularly.

When we were children, we called it play. Often, as adults we think of it as work. Since many adults feel and are overworked, it is no wonder large numbers of us avoid regular exercise.

While 30 minutes of aerobic exercise 3-4 times per week is heart healthy, 50-60 minutes 5-6 times per week promotes brain plasticity – the ability to develop new brain cells. Brain plasticity helps keep your brain sharp, thus assisting in creative thinking that, in turn, leads to more effective problem solving.

> **[Exercise assists] in creative thinking that, in turn, leads to more effective problem solving.**

Exercise also releases chemicals called endorphins into your blood stream to help fight off stress, depression and anxiety, and illness. Regular exercise helps you feel in a better frame of mind. It helps prevent chronic health problems that put the focus more on you than on your relationship.

To summarize, regular exercise keeps your body and mind healthy and sets you up for positive relationships. We marry "in sickness and in health." But "in health" is much easier on a relationship.

All adults are advised to have their health assessed by his or her physician before starting exercise, changing to a different type of exercise, or increasing the intensity of exercise. Be sure no physical reason exists to limit or avoid your chosen activity. It is self-defeating to put your health at risk by skipping this step.

You may be able to add a benefit to your exercise. As noted in Tip #24 *Spend quality time together,* many couples believe they don't have enough time to spend together. When schedules and preferred activity match, exercising companionably with your partner can be one way to enjoy more time together.

What fitness activity will you do to be physically, mentally, and relationally healthier today?

TIP #27
Read the best relationship guide ever written.

The Bible is the most complete book on relationships ever written. It is the #1 all time bestseller.

The Bible documents true stories ranging from the worst to the best in people and relationships. When taken in its whole context, it gives us the guidance we need to get along with ourselves and with others. It teaches us the following and so much more:

- the purpose and value of relationships,
- how to love,
- how to solve problems,
- how to sustain our values,
- how to be happy,
- how to handle anger,
- how to protect our relationships,
- how to forgive.

Top relationship love stories in the Bible to read include:

- Hosea and Gomer (Hosea 1-3),
- Abraham and Sarah (Genesis 12-23),
- Moses and Zipporah (Exodus 2, 4, 18; Numbers 12),
- Zechariah and Elizabeth (Luke 1-2),
- Jacob and Rachel (Genesis 29-30),
- Joseph and Mary (Matthew 1-2, Luke 1-2).

Other recommended reading includes, but isn't limited to, Proverbs, a book of wisdom in the Old Testament, and the parables of Jesus found in the Gospel section (the books Matthew, Mark, Luke, and John) of the New Testament.

The Bible is the most complete book on relationships ever written.

The Bible is translated into many versions and paraphrases. Choosing one can overwhelm you. Consider a *Life Application* Bible. It has extensive footnotes to help you relate what happened thousands of years ago to your life today. Remember to get the big picture. Focusing on one section alone, taking it out of context, can backfire on you and your relationships.

Are your most important relationships worth reading and understanding the best relationship guide ever written? Will you make it a habit to read and learn from the Bible, starting today?

TIP #28
Seek solutions to relationship conflict sooner, instead of later.

The longer an issue goes unresolved, the more pain and hopelessness grow. While this sounds like another no-brainer, it is surprising how often we neglect and put off taking care of our relationship needs.

No matter the type of problem or issue, often at first we are hopeful it will pass if we do nothing. We tend to take a let-me-see-what-tomorrow-brings attitude. This approach does work sometimes. In relationships, being proactive, "nipping it in the bud," prevents a smaller issue from becoming a bigger issue or growing out of control.

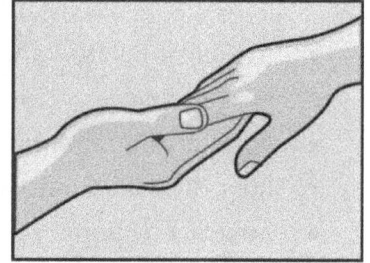

We know a small problem is easier to fix than a big one. That is why maintenance and care at regular intervals for most things, for example, our cars, our homes, and our bodies, is recommended. The price of neglect is greater financial expense, greater inconvenience, and greater stress.

> ...being proactive, "nipping it in the bud," prevents a smaller issue from becoming a bigger issue...

The same is true with the important people in our lives. The more we ignore maintenance and care of a relationship and delay seeking solutions to relationship conflicts, the more pain and hopelessness we experience. The more likely we are to give up. Along with greater unhappiness, again, the price of neglect is greater financial expense, greater inconvenience, and greater stress.

Do you have a relationship conflict you have avoided solving? What tips in this book look most helpful and hopeful to you for solving this conflict?

What step towards finding a healthy solution will you take today before the problem gets worse?

TIP #29
Have hope.

Even the best relationships are not problem-free. During times of relationship conflict, hold on to hope.

Building and maintaining a healthy relationship does not happen automatically, and it doesn't happen by accident. It takes commitment and effort. It is normal for committed relationships to have struggles. A relationship without conflict is a fantasy.

In the middle of ongoing conflict, you might become so discouraged you forget what you liked about the other person in the first place. You might decide you never really liked that person, you just thought you did. When focused on your bad feelings, you might rewrite your relationship history, forgetting or leaving out your collection of good memories.

You can choose the outcome of your struggles. You can choose to stay in a relationship and be miserable. You can walk away. Or you can choose hope and address your struggles by working out what is solvable and learning to accept peaceably the irreconcilable differences *all* relationships have.

When you need it, seek good relationship education and counseling from someone specially trained in teaching you proven successful relationship tools. Choose someone who gives you hope. Be cautious of family, friends, and therapists/counselors who tell you your

What will you do to increase your hope today?

relationship is dead and the best thing to do is get out of it. They are not in a position to decide what is best for you. Only you can examine your situation and values and decide what is best for you.

Seek out others who have hope, who have experience in turning around their own relationship problems, or in helping others turn around relationship problems.

What will you do and whom will you seek out when you need hope? Will you make a plan today, write it down, and put it where you can find it when you need hope?

What do you need to increase your hope about now? Are you using the tools in this book? Are you seeking out other ways to have hope for your relationship?

What will you do to increase your hope today?

35

TIP #30
Celebrate life together!

Is your glass half-empty or half-full? This isn't the first time you are asked this question in this book.

Do you focus on the negative – what is wrong, what you don't like, or what you don't have? When you do, you see your glass as half-empty. Do you focus on the positive – what is right, what you like, and what you do have? When you do, you see your glass as half-full. Where you put your focus affects your experiences and choices.

Watch the news and you become acutely aware of all that is wrong in our world, our country, our communities, our homes, and our relationships. Because "news" in the media is mostly bad news, we are fed a regular diet of half-empty.

Much is missing and is wrong in this world. We have war, hunger, disease, crime, abuse, and hate. That's only the beginning of a very long list.

What about good news? It's out there. You only have to notice. Kristen and Mike's baby boy arrived into the world fully formed, pink and healthy. Kristen is doing well. The blackberries are ripe on the vine, sweet, juicy, and abundant. Peg is busy picking the fruit and baking her famous blackberry pies to share with family and neighborhood friends. The airplane left on schedule, flew uneventfully across the country, and delivered its passengers safely and on time at their destination airport. Tom and Beth used humor to avoid an argument. This, too, is only the beginning of a very long list.

There's so much to be thankful for!

Look around you. Open your eyes to all that is right in the world, your country, your community, your home, and your relationships. Share abundantly the good in the world with the ones you hold dear in your heart, as well as the stranger you encounter on the street. Tip the first domino in a positive direction (see Tip #18 *Start chain reactions of positive events*). Go ahead, make their day!

You can feed on a regular diet of half-full. It is a healthy, nourishing, relationship-enhancing diet. Close your eyes, pause for a moment, and imagine what it would be like if we all did this. There's so much to be thankful for!

How and with whom will you celebrate life today?

FORWARD
Your journey doesn't end here.

Your journey to relationship health doesn't end here. Now it is time to retrace your steps.

Your journey to relationship health doesn't end here.

This book has given you 30 concrete tips to healthier relationships. Having the right tips is an important start. However, they are only as good as what you choose to do with them.

Reading these tips 10, 100, or 1000 times won't change your relationship(s). You create relationship health by taking action that works. The Workbook that follows is the larger section of *30 Tips to Healthier Relationships*. Consider its size a measure of its importance to you. It is your guide for action to successful results.

Although you have to do the work, it doesn't have to be *hard* work. It does have to be *smart* work. The workbook's design is a tool to ease your way to work smart.

You *can* make these tips work for you! If you haven't started using the Workbook, I recommend you start today. Use it as tool for planning, monitoring and reviewing your success.

Turn the page. Take the next step in your journey to relationship health. I dare you!

Workbook

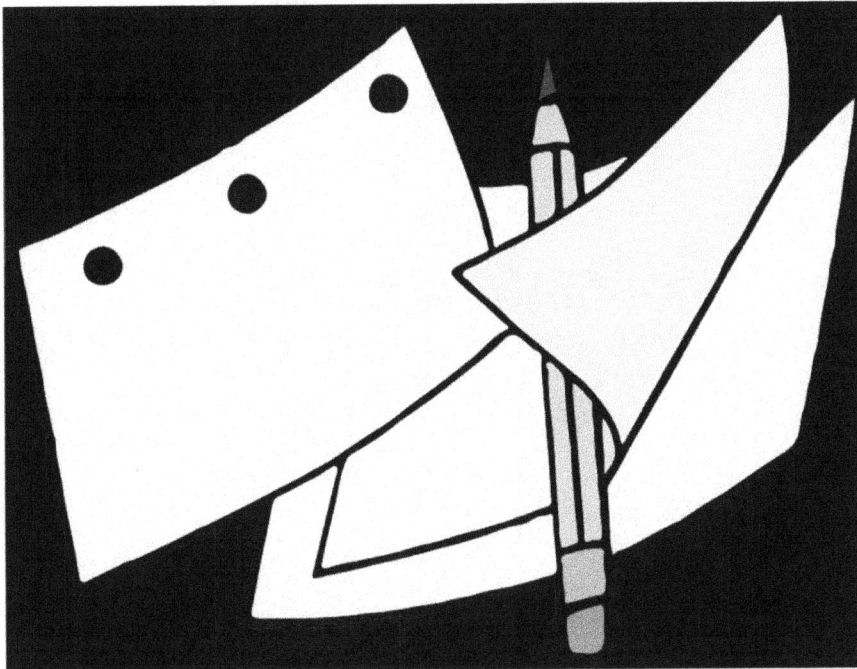

Choosing what you want to do, making a plan for what you will do, and keeping track of your progress as you do it, is an excellent strategy for success. I strongly urge you to use this workbook to help you with the challenge of improving your relationship(s). It is a tool to ease your way to relationship health as you work through these 30 Tips.

The strategy:
- It is essential you write your goals in a positive way – what you want to happen, instead of a negative way – what you want to stop happening.
- The more specific, action-oriented, and concrete you are about the goals you set, the more likely you will reach your desired outcome. Include:
  - your goal(s),
  - how you will accomplish your goal(s), and
  - the roadblocks you are likely to encounter along the way.
- Choose small, manageable goals.
- Tweak your plan until you have the results you want.

These are proven ways to get great results. If you don't have enough room to write your responses in the space provided, it's OK to use more paper!

Look at the sample worksheet for Tip #1. It shows you how you can use your workbook. Then, fill out a worksheet with your own plan. Try it. Then, where needed, you are welcome to modify anything in the workbook to better suit your needs.

You have space to record information on each Tip for three weeks. This gives you the chance to
- figure out what it is you want,
- make a plan of action,
- try out your plan,
- evaluate your results,
- change anything that isn't working, or just tweak it a bit, and
- keep doing what works.

If you get the results you want in less than three weeks, great. If you need more than three weeks to achieve these results, continue until you are successful. Revise and fine-tune as many times as it takes to reach the success you want. There is no magic in the number three.

Expect that some tips will be easy for you, while others will be more challenging and take more time to accomplish. This is normal.

The Workbook asks the basic questions. If you want or need to break these questions down into more detail, here are some additional questions to ask yourself.

- Where did I experience clear success?
- Where did I experience partial success?
- What did I do that worked that I am still doing?
- What did I do that worked and I have stopped doing?
- Why did I stop?
- Will I start again?
- When will I start again?
- What didn't work?
- Why do I think it didn't work?
- What could I try differently?
- Will I try this different thing?
- When will I try this different thing?
- What could benefit me to do I haven't yet done?
- What stops me?
- How important is it for me to find a workable solution?
- What steps will I take to find this solution?
- What is my reaction to my changes?
- What is my partner's reaction to my changes?
- What changes have I observed in our relationship?
- What is my next step to improve our relationship?
- Will I take this step?
- When will I take this step?
- Where do I feel hopeless?
- Where do I feel hope?
- Who is in my life that can carry hope for me when I feel hopeless?

Relationships require ongoing attention. When you stop doing what works and slip back into old, unproductive or destructive habits, your relationship, predictably, takes that unwanted downward spiral. Most people will value from reviewing their notes in this workbook regularly. A well-timed review can be a great way to stay on the road to healthy relationship success.

You can do this! You can use this book and this workbook to make a lasting, healthy difference in the relationship(s) you treasure most. Start now!

SAMPLE WORKSHEET   **Tip #1**
Share verbal appreciation every day.

Week 1: Try It

The experiment I
will do:

> I will share, with words, at least one appreciation
> with my husband, Mike, every day.

The results I want
from using this tip:

> I want to feel better about Mike by noticing the
> good things he says and does. I want him to hear I
> notice. I want him to want to be home and be
> around me.

What I will do that
will set me up for
success:

> I will say my appreciation in a conversational voice
> (in a way that is not flashy, dramatic, or showy).
> Using a few short sentences, I will tell Mike why I
> appreciate what he said or did.

Ways I can set
myself up to be
unsuccessful:

> I can get so irritated with Mike I decide not to tell
> him an appreciation. I can decide to forget to tell
> him. I can use too many words. I can get angry
> when I don't get the kind of response I want from
> him.

After Week 1: How did I do?

What happened:

I started to do what I think is the right thing – to use words to share appreciations with Mike. I got angry when I didn't hear any appreciation of me from him, and so I ended up starting an argument a couple of times. One time, though, after I shared an appreciation with words, he hugged me!

What I will continue doing:

I will share a verbal appreciation with Mike every day for another week, even if I feel discouraged or angry because of what he does or doesn't do in return.

What I will do differently:

When I don't notice getting an appreciation back, I will practice slowing my thinking down by taking some deep breaths, instead of getting angry and starting a fight. (It's hard to give appreciations and not get them back.) I can use too many words. I'll share appreciations clearly, using fewer words.

Where I need more information or help, and what I will do to get it:

I will ask Sarah if it is OK if I talk with her about what I want to do, rehearse with her the appreciation I want to share with Mike until we agree it sounds right, and tell her my successes and where I trip up.

After week 2: Sticking with it

What happened:

I stuck to my decision to focus on sharing an appreciation with Mike every day using words. Several times, he left the room. Once when he didn't leave the room he turned his head, but I could see he smiled. We are arguing less!

What I learned works:

I put this tip on my computer Desktop. Seeing it every day reminds me to do it. It works when I stick to the formula in this book for sharing verbal appreciations. I need to make sure Mike is listening (not in the middle of a project or TV show), when I share my appreciation.

What I learned doesn't work:

It doesn't work if I over-explain my appreciation. Mike stops listening. Following my appreciation with a complaint (but I don't like it when you...) doesn't work either. It spoils my appreciation.

My next step(s):

I'll keep sharing at least one verbal appreciation a day with Mike. I'll know from his reaction if I need to change something. If what I do stops working, I'll talk to Sarah about what I need to do differently. I'll avoid doing what I know doesn't work. I'm going to pick another tip to try.

Tip #1
Share verbal appreciation every day.

Week 1: Try It

The experiment I will do:

The results I want from using this tip:

What I will do that will set me up for success:

Ways I can set myself up to be unsuccessful:

After Week 1: How did I do?

What happened:

What I will
continue doing:

What I will do
differently:

Where I need
more information
or help, and what
I will do to get it:

After week 2: Sticking with it

What happened:

What I learned
works:

What I learned
doesn't work:

My next step(s):

Tip #2
Recognize and share non-verbal appreciation.

Week 1: Try It

The experiment I
will do:

The results I want
from using this tip:

What I will do that
will set me up for
success:

Ways I can set
myself up to be
unsuccessful:

After Week 1: How did I do?

What happened:

What I will
continue doing:

What I will do
differently:

Where I need
more information
or help, and what
I will do to get it:

After week 2: Sticking with it

What happened:

What I learned
works:

What I learned
doesn't work:

My next step(s):

Tip #3
When someone talks to you, focus on what he or she is saying.

Week 1: Try It

The experiment I will do:

The results I want from using this tip:

What I will do that will set me up for success:

Ways I can set myself up to be unsuccessful:

After Week 1: How did I do?

What happened:

What I will
continue doing:

What I will do
differently:

Where I need
more information
or help, and what
I will do to get it:

After week 2: Sticking with it

What happened:

What I learned
works:

What I learned
doesn't work:

My next step(s):

Tip #4
Treat another's concerns seriously.

Week 1: Try It

The experiment I will do:

The results I want from using this tip:

What I will do that will set me up for success:

Ways I can set myself up to be unsuccessful:

After Week 1: How did I do?

What happened:

What I will
continue doing:

What I will do
differently:

Where I need
more information
or help, and what
I will do to get it:

After week 2: Sticking with it

What happened:

What I learned
works:

What I learned
doesn't work:

My next step(s):

Tip #5
Ask permission, and get it, before offering advice.

Week 1: Try It

The experiment I will do:

The results I want from using this tip:

What I will do that will set me up for success:

Ways I can set myself up to be unsuccessful:

After Week 1: How did I do?

What happened:

What I will
continue doing:

What I will do
differently:

Where I need
more information
or help, and what
I will do to get it:

After week 2: Sticking with it

What happened:

What I learned
works:

What I learned
doesn't work:

My next step(s):

Tip #6
Practice goodwill.

Week 1: Try It

The experiment I
will do:

The results I want
from using this tip:

What I will do that
will set me up for
success:

Ways I can set
myself up to be
unsuccessful:

After Week 1: How did I do?

What happened:

What I will
continue doing:

What I will do
differently:

Where I need
more information
or help, and what
I will do to get it:

After week 2: Sticking with it

What happened:

My next step(s):

What I learned
works:

What I learned
doesn't work:

My next step(s):

Tip #7
Make choices based on what you value, rather than what you feel.

Week 1: Try It

The experiment I
will do:

The results I want
from using this tip:

What I will do that
will set me up for
success:

Ways I can set
myself up to be
unsuccessful:

After Week 1: How did I do?

What happened:

What I will
continue doing:

What I will do
differently:

Where I need
more information
or help, and what
I will do to get it:

After week 2: Sticking with it

What happened:

What I learned
works:

What I learned
doesn't work:

My next step(s):

Tip #8
Be careful on Facebook.

Week 1: Try It

The experiment I will do:

The results I want from using this tip:

What I will do that will set me up for success:

Ways I can set myself up to be unsuccessful:

After Week 1: How did I do?

What happened:

What I will
continue doing:

What I will do
differently:

Where I need
more information
or help, and what
I will do to get it:

After week 2: Sticking with it

What happened:

What I learned
works:

What I learned
doesn't work:

My next step(s):

Tip #9
Make having satisfying relationships a priority over being right.
Week 1: Try It

The experiment I will do:

The results I want from using this tip:

What I will do that will set me up for success:

Ways I can set myself up to be unsuccessful:

69

After Week 1: How did I do?

What happened:

What I will
continue doing:

What I will do
differently:

Where I need
more information
or help, and what
I will do to get it:

After week 2: Sticking with it

What happened:

What I learned works:

What I learned doesn't work:

My next step(s):

Tip #10
Look for the exceptions to problems.

Week 1: Try It

The experiment I
will do:

The results I want
from using this tip:

What I will do that
will set me up for
success:

Ways I can set
myself up to be
unsuccessful:

After Week 1: How did I do?

What happened:

What I will
continue doing:

What I will do
differently:

Where I need
more information
or help, and what
I will do to get it:

After week 2: Sticking with it

What happened:

What I learned
works:

What I learned
doesn't work:

My next step(s):

Tip #11
Be trustworthy.

Week 1: Try It

The experiment I
will do:

The results I want
from using this tip:

What I will do that
will set me up for
success:

Ways I can set
myself up to be
unsuccessful:

After Week 1: How did I do?

What happened:

What I will
continue doing:

What I will do
differently:

Where I need
more information
or help, and what
I will do to get it:

After week 2: Sticking with it

What happened:

What I learned
works:

What I learned
doesn't work:

My next step(s):

Tip #12
Avoid blaming.

Week 1: Try It

The experiment I
will do:

The results I want
from using this tip:

What I will do that
will set me up for
success:

Ways I can set
myself up to be
unsuccessful:

After Week 1: How did I do?

What happened:

What I will
continue doing:

What I will do
differently:

Where I need
more information
or help, and what
I will do to get it:

After week 2: Sticking with it

What happened:

What I learned
works:

What I learned
doesn't work:

My next step(s):

Tip #13
Look for the best in people.

Week 1: Try It

The experiment I will do:

The results I want from using this tip:

What I will do that will set me up for success:

Ways I can set myself up to be unsuccessful:

After Week 1: How did I do?

What happened:

What I will
continue doing:

What I will do
differently:

Where I need
more information
or help, and what
I will do to get it:

After week 2: Sticking with it

What happened:

What I learned works:

What I learned doesn't work:

My next step(s):

Tip #14
Take a time out.

Week 1: Try It

The experiment I
will do:

The results I want
from using this tip:

What I will do that
will set me up for
success:

Ways I can set
myself up to be
unsuccessful:

After Week 1: How did I do?

What happened:

What I will
continue doing:

What I will do
differently:

Where I need
more information
or help, and what
I will do to get it:

After week 2: Sticking with it

What happened:

What I learned
works:

What I learned
doesn't work:

My next step(s):

Tip #15
Express complaints privately.

Week 1: Try It

The experiment I will do:

The results I want from using this tip:

What I will do that will set me up for success:

Ways I can set myself up to be unsuccessful:

After Week 1: How did I do?

What happened:

What I will
continue doing:

What I will do
differently:

Where I need
more information
or help, and what
I will do to get it:

After week 2: Sticking with it

What happened:

What I learned
works:

What I learned
doesn't work:

My next step(s):

Tip #16
Make your most important relationship a higher priority than you.
Week 1: Try It

The experiment I will do:

The results I want from using this tip:

What I will do that will set me up for success:

Ways I can set myself up to be unsuccessful:

After Week 1: How did I do?

What happened:

What I will
continue doing:

What I will do
differently:

Where I need
more information
or help, and what
I will do to get it:

After week 2: Sticking with it

What happened:

What I learned
works:

What I learned
doesn't work:

My next step(s):

Tip #17
When you make a mistake, ask for forgiveness.

Week 1: Try It

The experiment I will do:

The results I want from using this tip:

What I will do that will set me up for success:

Ways I can set myself up to be unsuccessful:

After Week 1: How did I do?

What happened:

What I will
continue doing:

What I will do
differently:

Where I need
more information
or help, and what
I will do to get it:

After week 2: Sticking with it

What happened:

What I learned works:

What I learned doesn't work:

My next step(s):

Tip #18
Start chain reactions of positive events.

Week 1: Try It

The experiment I
will do:

The results I want
from using this tip:

What I will do that
will set me up for
success:

Ways I can set
myself up to be
unsuccessful:

After Week 1: How did I do?

What happened:

What I will
continue doing:

What I will do
differently:

Where I need
more information
or help, and what
I will do to get it:

After week 2: Sticking with it

What happened:

What I learned works:

What I learned doesn't work:

My next step(s):

Tip #19
Practice good sleep habits.

Week 1: Try It

The experiment I will do:

(blank box)

The results I want from using this tip:

(blank box)

What I will do that will set me up for success:

(blank box)

Ways I can set myself up to be unsuccessful:

(blank box)

After Week 1: How did I do?

What happened:

What I will
continue doing:

What I will do
differently:

Where I need
more information
or help, and what
I will do to get it:

After week 2: Sticking with it

What happened:

What I learned works:

What I learned doesn't work:

My next step(s):

Tip #20
Avoid resentments.

Week 1: Try It

The experiment I
will do:

The results I want
from using this tip:

What I will do that
will set me up for
success:

Ways I can set
myself up to be
unsuccessful:

After Week 1: How did I do?

What happened:

What I will
continue doing:

What I will do
differently:

Where I need
more information
or help, and what
I will do to get it:

After week 2: Sticking with it

What happened:

What I learned
works:

What I learned
doesn't work:

My next step(s):

Tip #21
Choose the best time to bring up a problem.

Week 1: Try It

The experiment I will do:

The results I want from using this tip:

What I will do that will set me up for success:

Ways I can set myself up to be unsuccessful:

After Week 1: How did I do?

What happened:

What I will
continue doing:

What I will do
differently:

Where I need
more information
or help, and what
I will do to get it:

After week 2: Sticking with it

What happened:

What I learned works:

What I learned doesn't work:

My next step(s):

Tip #22
Live from this day forward.

Week 1: Try It

The experiment I
will do:

The results I want
from using this tip:

What I will do that
will set me up for
success:

Ways I can set
myself up to be
unsuccessful:

108

After Week 1: How did I do?

What happened:

What I will
continue doing:

What I will do
differently:

Where I need
more information
or help, and what
I will do to get it:

After week 2: Sticking with it

What happened:

What I learned
works:

What I learned
doesn't work:

My next step(s):

Tip #23
Be a successful mind reader.

Week 1: Try It

The experiment I
will do:

The results I want
from using this tip:

What I will do that
will set me up for
success:

Ways I can set
myself up to be
unsuccessful:

After Week 1: How did I do?

What happened:

What I will
continue doing:

What I will do
differently:

Where I need
more information
or help, and what
I will do to get it:

After week 2: Sticking with it

What happened:

What I learned
works:

What I learned
doesn't work:

My next step(s):

Tip #24
Spend quality time together.

Week 1: Try It

The experiment I will do:

The results I want from using this tip:

What I will do that will set me up for success:

Ways I can set myself up to be unsuccessful:

After Week 1: How did I do?

What happened:

What I will
continue doing:

What I will do
differently:

Where I need
more information
or help, and what
I will do to get it:

After week 2: Sticking with it

What happened:

What I learned
works:

What I learned
doesn't work:

My next step(s):

Tip #25
Take a break from your relationship problem.

Week 1: Try It

The experiment I will do:

The results I want from using this tip:

What I will do that will set me up for success:

Ways I can set myself up to be unsuccessful:

After Week 1: How did I do?

What happened:

What I will
continue doing:

What I will do
differently:

Where I need
more information
or help, and what
I will do to get it:

After week 2: Sticking with it

What happened:

What I learned works:

What I learned doesn't work:

My next step(s):

Tip #26
Exercise regularly.

Week 1: Try It

The experiment I will do:

The results I want from using this tip:

What I will do that will set me up for success:

Ways I can set myself up to be unsuccessful:

After Week 1: How did I do?

What happened:

What I will
continue doing:

What I will do
differently:

Where I need
more information
or help, and what
I will do to get it:

After week 2: Sticking with it

What happened:

What I learned
works:

What I learned
doesn't work:

My next step(s):

Tip #27
Read the best relationship guide ever written.

Week 1: Try It

The experiment I will do:

The results I want from using this tip:

What I will do that will set me up for success:

Ways I can set myself up to be unsuccessful:

After Week 1: How did I do?

What happened:

What I will
continue doing:

What I will do
differently:

Where I need
more information
or help, and what
I will do to get it:

After week 2: Sticking with it

What happened:

What I learned
works:

What I learned
doesn't work:

My next step(s):

Tip #28
Seek solutions to relationship conflict sooner, instead of later.
Week 1: Try It

The experiment I
will do:

The results I want
from using this tip:

What I will do that
will set me up for
success:

Ways I can set
myself up to be
unsuccessful:

After Week 1: How did I do?

What happened:

What I will
continue doing:

What I will do
differently:

Where I need
more information
or help, and what
I will do to get it:

After week 2: Sticking with it

What happened:

What I learned
works:

What I learned
doesn't work:

My next step(s):

Tip #29
Have hope.

Week 1: Try It

The experiment I
will do:

[ ]

The results I want
from using this tip:

[ ]

What I will do that
will set me up for
success:

[ ]

Ways I can set
myself up to be
unsuccessful:

[ ]

After Week 1: How did I do?

What happened:

What I will
continue doing:

What I will do
differently:

Where I need
more information
or help, and what
I will do to get it:

After week 2: Sticking with it

What happened:

What I learned
works:

What I learned
doesn't work:

My next step(s):

Tip #30
Celebrate life together!

Week 1: Try It

The experiment I will do:

The results I want from using this tip:

What I will do that will set me up for success:

Ways I can set myself up to be unsuccessful:

After Week 1: How did I do?

What happened:

What I will
continue doing:

What I will do
differently:

Where I need
more information
or help, and what
I will do to get it:

After week 2: Sticking with it

What happened:

What I learned works:

What I learned doesn't work:

My next step(s):

AUTHOR'S "HOPE TALK"

The rewards for creating healthier relationships are awesome. While following these 30 tips will not eliminate all relationship problems, it can help you heal and prevent relationship conflicts. It can help you make smart decisions for how to handle problems when they inevitably arise.

By creating healthier relationships, you feel better about yourself, your partner, and other people in your life. You discover your partner and others feel better about you, and probably about themselves. With your first action, you start that domino effect. You discover most relationship problems are solvable, and how to live in relative peace with the ones that are not.

You can wake up in the morning looking forward to the promise of a new day. You can look forward to the company and companionship of your partner. You can lay your head on your pillow at the end of the day, and drift off to sleep smiling with contentment. What a way to live!

My passion is creating and keeping healthy relationships. I invite you to make it yours.

Let me know your success stories. I am eager to hear them. I invite you to send them to me by email at jenny.lightedpathways@gmail.com.

To your relationship success!
Jenny Olin, MSW, LCSW

Website: www.HealthyRelationshipsForLife.com
Blog: http://CreatingHealthyRelationships.wordpress.com

www.ingramcontent.com/pod-product-compliance
Lightning Source LLC
Chambersburg PA
CBHW080051280326
41934CB00014B/3276